DEVELOPI   MOBILE APPLIC..... .... WITH IONIC AND ANGULAR

IONIC AND ANGULAR: IDEA TO APP STORE, BOOK ONE

By

MICHAEL D. CALLAGHAN

walkingriver.com

Other Books by Michael Callaghan

Developing Progressive Web Applications with Angular (and Ionic): How to Build and Deploy Mobile Applications without Paying Apple or Google for the Privilege

Developing a Mobile Application UI with Ionic and React: How to Build Your First Mobile Application with Common Web Technologies

Sign up at https://walkingriver.com to receive advanced notice and occasional rough-draft content of new books in this series.

Online Courses by Michael Callaghan

Pluralsight

Over the past few years, I have authored four popular Ionic courses for Pluralsight, which you can find here: http://bit.ly/ps-mike

Other Courses

I have two Ionic courses coming soon or available now at Udemy. They are companions to this book series.

- Ionic and React: Building a Mobile Application UI
- Ionic and Angular: Building a Mobile Application UI (Coming Soon)

Sign up at https://walkingriver.com to receive discount codes and advanced notice of new courses.

Introduction

I have been using the Ionic Framework for mobile application development since 2014, before it was even officially released. Since then, Ionic has been my go-to technology for building mobile apps. With the release of version four in 2019, Ionic grew beyond its humble origins as an angular-based framework for making mobile apps. Today, Ionic works with a variety of web technologies. It has become a first-class citizen for building all manner of web applications.

The Ionic Framework supports a variety of mobile platforms. Throughout this series, I will cover the important aspects of development with Ionic and Angular, going from the initial idea all the way to the Apple App and Google Play Stores.

This volume will cover the absolute basics: I will show you how to build a simple Ionic application. I will cover the application structure, explaining how an Ionic application is laid out. Next, I will introduce some of Ionic's more useful UI components and create a basic side-menu for the demo application.

Unlike many books that spend a lot of time on background, this one is designed to be fast paced, with a minimum of fuss and fluff. It is all hands-on.

I expect you to have some basic understanding of web development. You should know what a <div> is, for example, and know how to create a button. You should have a decent grasp of JavaScript, but you do not need to be a master.

I do not expect you to have ever used Angular or the Ionic Framework, but it certainly will not hurt you if you have. I should make clear that this is not a book on Angular. While I will point out basic aspects of Angular as they pertain to Ionic, I will not go any deeper than I must to make the demo application work.

Concepts will be explained as needed, as close to their use as I can get.

By the time you complete the series, you should have the confidence you need to create and deploy your own mobile app for iOS or Android.

It will be a fast ride, so hang on.

Road Map

This is the first in what I plan to be a series of books on developing applications with Ionic and Angular.

Book 1: Building a Mobile Application UI

This book is all about building a user interface for a mobile application from scratch. It contains everything you need to go from nothing to a fully functional mobile app UI with Ionic Framework and Angular. Many of Ionic's basic UI components will be showcased:

- Ion-card
- Ion-item
- Ion-button
- Ion-icon
- Ion-menu
- Ion-alert
- Ion-option-sliding
- Ion-action-sheet
- And More

Book 2: Dealing with Data

Once the basic user interface is complete, it is time to work with data. How will the application accept, validate, and store user-provided input? This book will answer those questions.

When the application functionality is completed, it still needs to be available to its potential users. The final section of this book will be a discussion around various hosting options. You will deploy the application as a Progressive Web Application, which can then be installed on any modern mobile device.

Book 3: Devices and Deployment

Sometimes, you need true hardware integration and installation. In this book, you will work with Capacitor, Ionic's solution for interfacing with the mobile hardware.

The book will conclude by explaining and demonstrating how to prepare, build, and deploy the finished application to both the Apple and Google Play Stores.

Table of Contents

Getting Started

Prerequisites

Primarily, you will need a decent text-editor, or integrated developer environment. I use and recommend Visual Studio Code. VS Code is a free and open-source cross-platform development environment for Microsoft, designed from the ground-up to work with all the technologies you will be using. Of course, you are free to use whatever tool you are comfortable with.

Software Tools

Developing and deploying an Ionic application require some initial configuration. You will need the following tools, in addition to the code editor:

- Node
- NPM
- Git
- The Ionic CLI itself, installed globally

Most of the tools you will use rely on Node, a JavaScript-based runtime environment. I recommend the LTS, or long-term-support version.

NPM is a package manager built on top of node. Most of the tools you need are distributed as npm packages. It is installed with node.

Most of the tutorials for Ionic expect you to have Git, a powerful and flexible source control system, and its related tools. If you have a Mac or Linux, you probably already have it.

Quite frankly, that is about it. Installing these items depends on your platform.

If you need detailed instructions on how to do that, refer to the Appendix – Installing the Tools.

Demo Code

The demo code accompanying this book is available on GitHub, tagged for each book. Find this book's code at https://github.com/walkingriver/at10dance-angular/tree/volume1-demo.

Gentle Introduction to Angular

As I said before, this is not a book on Angular. However, there are some patterns and syntax idioms I want to introduce early before you get into the code. I like to think of them as Angularisms (yes, I just made up that word).

To work through the example in this chapter, open a browser to https://stackblitz.com/fork/angular This will provide you with an immediate sandbox where you can follow along. As soon as you do, you should see the following code in the center panel, a file call app.component.ts.

```
import { Component } from '@angular/core';

@Component({
  selector: 'my-app',
  templateUrl: './app.component.html',
  styleUrls: [ './app.component.css' ]
})
export class AppComponent  {
  name = 'Angular';
}
```

Let us start by talking about Angular's concept of separation of concerns. In Angular, UI functionality is encapsulated in components. A component can represent anything from a piece of text, a button, a form, or even an entire page. Components can contain other components, and they can communicate with each other through well-defined interfaces.

You specify that a TypeScript class is a component using the @component decorator. Decorators provide additional information by annotating or modifying classes or class members.

In this case, the component decorator provides additional metadata to Angular about how the class will behave.

The selector attribute tells angular to expose this component using the html tag <my-app>.

The templateUrl attribute indicates that the HTML markup can be found in the file specified, app.component.html.

Likewise, with the styleUrls. Notice that this value is an array, which means you can provide more than one CSS file.

If you look on the left-hand panel, you should see both of these files.

The executable portion of the component code is found inside the class definition. This one contains a single line of code, meaning it is not doing much.

This is what you mean by a "separation of concerns." The code, markup, and styles are all separated from one another.

 take a look at the markup, which is found in the template file, app.component.html. This file is pure HTML containing the content.

```
<hello name="{{ name }}"></hello>
<p>
  Start editing to see some magic happen :)
</p>
```

Notice the first line contains another custom HTML tag, <hello>. That is defined in hello.component.ts, which you will review shortly.

Inside of that tag is an attribute called name, set to the value {{ name }}. This is an Angular "one-way" binding expression. During the page rendering phase, Angular sees that expression, and knows to set the value of the name attribute to the run-time value of the variable name on the component. It would probably be less confusing if they used a different variable name.

Return to the component code and change the name variable. I changed mine to look like this.

```
export class AppComponent  {
  name = 'Mike';
}
```

Look at the result that appears in the right-hand pane. The value you provided should be displayed instead of the original value.

Hello Mike!

Start editing to see some magic happen :)

Open up the file hello.component.ts and look at its implementation. You first thing you may notice is that all of its markup and styling is defined in the same file.

```
import { Component, Input } from '@angular/core';

@Component({
  selector: 'hello',
  template: `<h1>Hello {{name}}!</h1>`,
  styles: [`h1 { font-family: Lato; }`]
})
export class HelloComponent  {
  @Input() name: string;
}
```

Instead of providing a templateUrl and styleUrls, both of them are provided directly in the file. It is worth pointing out that this is still a form of separation of concerns. The HTML markup is clearly separated from the styling and component code.

Personally, I would not recommend you do this, except in the simplest of components. That said, there are many proponents of keeping all of your component code in one file. Find your own balance; it is probably somewhere in between "always" and "never" doing this.

Inside the component code is a single line of code.

```
@Input() name: string;
```

The @Input decorator specifies that name is a string attribute that can be provided in the markup of any client that uses this component.

Component Reuse

The real power behind this is that you can reuse the component anywhere, simply replacing its name attribute, and it will render consistently.

Back in app.component.html, make a few copies of the <hello> tag and provide different names. Something like this, perhaps.

```
<hello name="{{ name }}"></hello>
<hello name="Greg"></hello>
<hello name="Jonathan"></hello>
<hello name="Neil"></hello>
<p>
   Start editing to see some magic happen :)
</p>
```

Now it looks like this, and I do not have be concerned with how the <hello> tag works behind the scenes. I can simply reuse it.

Hello Mike!

Hello Greg!

Hello Jonathan!

Hello Neil!

Start editing to see some magic happen :)

ngFor

But what if you have a bunch of names? Change the name variable on the component and make it an array called names.

```
export class AppComponent {
  names = ['Mike', 'Greg', 'Jonathan', 'Neil'];
}
```

The cool thing about reusing components this way is that you do not have to change the hello component at all. You simply need to change the calling code to use ngFor, an Angular directive used to create multiple instances of the hello component based on the number of elements in the referenced array.

You use an ngFor by providing it as an attribute to the element you want replicated. The value inside the quotes is the looping expression. It consists of the keyword *let* followed by the variable name to be used inside the element and any of its children, the keyword *of*, and the name of the array on the component to loop over.

```
<hello *ngFor="let name of names" name="{{name}}"></hello>
```

The asterisk, which is required, is an indication to Angular that this directive will manipulate the DOM, or the page's document object model, in some way.

Attribute Binding

There is another Binding syntax that works with HTML attributes. If you want to set the value of an attribute to a value on your component, use square brackets around the attribute name.

```
<hello *ngFor="let name of names" [name]="name"></hello>
```

Here, name, in square brackets, refers to the HTML attribute of the custom component. The other name, in quotes, is the name of the variable in the ngFor expression. When you are binding to an HTML attribute, this is my preferred method because you can run just about any code you want inside of those quotes.

HTML Event Binding

You can also bind to HTML events. Any event can become a trigger to execute a function on the component. The simplest way to illustrate that is to create a button and provide a click handler.

You do that by surrounding the event name (in this case, click) with parenthesis. Then inside the quotes, call the component function you want to execute.

You can pass parameters to the function, which is often the case when creating an event binding inside an *ngFor, passing the current looping variable to the event handler.

In this case, just call toggle().

```
<button (click)="toggle()">Click Me</button>
```

Back inside the component, you need to implement the toggle function. Add this code inside the app component, right after the names array.

```
isToggled = false;

toggle() {
  this.isToggled = !this.isToggled;
}
```

Now when you click the toggle button, the value of the isToggled variable will flip between true and false.

ngIf

The isToggled variable is useless until you do something with it. Add a new line inside the app component template file.

In this case, add a paragraph tag, give it an ngIf directive, and set it to "isToggled."

```
<p *ngIf="isToggled">
  I am toggled on!!!
</p>
```

ngIf will conditionally render the HTML tag if the value inside the quotes evaluates to a truthy value. Notice that ngIf also requires an asterisk because it modifies the DOM.

Hello Jonathan!

Hello Neil!

Start editing to see some magic happen :)

Click Me

Now as you click the button, that paragraph will appear and disappear.

Hello Jonathan!

Hello Neil!

Start editing to see some magic happen :)

Click Me

I am toggled on!!!

Those are the basics you need to know to work with Ionic and Angular Next, you will go ahead and create an Ionic app.

Your First Ionic App

One of the things I like to do in my home directory is have a folder called "git." You can call it anything you want: "projects," "myprojects," "ionic," it does not really matter.

Something I always do before starting an Ionic project is to ensure that I have the latest tooling, even if I just installed it yesterday. I recommend you do the same. Inside a command terminal of your choice, enter the following command:

```
npm install -g @ionic/cli@latest
```

Not surprisingly, this will ensure that you get the absolute latest version there is for us.

Ionic App Wizard

Through the rest of this book, I am going to stick to the command line, but Ionic has a web-based tool for building Ionic projects rapidly, called the Ionic App Wizard.

Try that right now and see what kind of project it provides. Open a browser to https://ionicframework.com/start. Supply a name, pick a color, and select the side-menu template. It appears to default to React, so make sure you select Angular.

On the next screen, sign in or create an account. Or you can choose to skip that and just get your results.

The wizard gives you a custom-install command for the Ionic CLI, and it warns you that you must have Ionic CLI 6.3 or above, which should not be an issue, but is why I always recommend having the latest version of the tooling.

Back in your terminal, run the command that the Ionic App Wizard gave you and wait. It will run an npm install, and then you will need to cd into that directory.

Enter the following command to launch the app.

```
ionic serve
```

It should automatically open in your default browser. The application it creates looks like an email box.

And voila! You just created an app out of nothing. In the next chapter, I will review the code it generated.

Guided Tour of the Ionic-Angular Code

For this tour, I am going to assume you are using Visual Studio Code. If not, you should still be able to follow along.

Open the project the Ionic App Wizard created using the command

```
code .
```

index.html

Every web application starts with index.html, right? Well, it is not always true, but it is the default with an Ionic-Angular app. Open index.html now.

At the top of the file are a bunch of HTML meta tags inside the page head. The folks at Ionic have already done the hard part of figuring these out, and I recommend that you not mess with them.

```
<body>
  <app-root></app-root>
</body>
```

The HTML body tag contains a single custom HTML element, app-root. That is the how the app is created. So, look at where app-root is defined.

app.component.ts

Open the file src/app/app.component.ts. This is where you will find app-root. In fact, this file should look similar to the one you saw on StackBlitz.

```
@Component({
    selector: 'app-root',
    templateUrl: 'app.component.html',
    styleUrls: ['app.component.scss']
})
```

To review, the component decorator near the top defines some
information about the component and how it should be rendered.
The selector tells Angular that the tag name will be app-root; the
HTML markup is in a file call app.component.html, which you
will see in a moment; and its custom styles are in
app.component.scss.

```
public selectedIndex = 0;
public appPages = [
    {
        title: 'Inbox',
        url: '/folder/Inbox',
        icon: 'mail'
    },
    {
        title: 'Outbox',
        url: '/folder/Outbox',
        icon: 'paper-plane'
    },
    {
        title: 'Favorites',
        url: '/folder/Favorites',
        icon: 'heart'
    },
    {
        title: 'Archived',
        url: '/folder/Archived',
        icon: 'archive'
    },
    {
        title: 'Trash',
        url: '/folder/Trash',
        icon: 'trash'
    },
    {
```

```
      title: 'Spam',
      url: '/folder/Spam',
      icon: 'warning'
    }
  ];
  public labels = ['Family', 'Friends', 'Notes', 'Work',
'Travel', 'Reminders'];
```

At the top of the class are some variables. There is a variable to hold the index of the selected page, followed by an array of Pages. So now you can see where those come from. Next come the labels you can see in the menu below the pages.

It is traditional in an Angular app to define all of the class level variables and fields near the top, followed by the class constructor, which is what you see next.

```
constructor(
    private platform: Platform,
    private splashScreen: SplashScreen,
    private statusBar: StatusBar
) {
    this.initializeApp();
}
```

In the parameter list to the constructor is where you can inject assorted services that the component will require: Platform, an Ionic service, provides various pieces of information about the device or platform the app is running on. The next two, SplashScreen and StatusBar, are specific to running on physical devices, which we will not cover here.

InitializeApp is a bit of boilerplate that I am going to ignore for now.

```
ngOnInit() {
  const path =
    window.location.pathname.split('folder/')[1];
```

```
if (path !== undefined) {
  this.selectedIndex = this.appPages.findIndex(page =>
    page.title.toLowerCase() === path.toLowerCase());
}
}
```

ngOnInit is what is known as an Angular lifecycle hook. There are a bunch of them, but this one is used pretty often. Angular will call ngOnInit once when the component and all of its children have been initialized. You put code in here that you want to run early, after any databinding. In this case, it is checking the URL of the current page to try to determine which page from the pages array that is currently being rendered.

app-routing.module

Next open src/app/app-routing.module.ts to see how to navigate to those pages. All of the main application routes are defined here.

```
const routes: Routes = [
  {
    path: '',
    redirectTo: 'folder/Inbox',
    pathMatch: 'full'
  },
  {
    path: 'folder/:id',
    loadChildren: () =>
      import('./folder/folder.module').then( m =>
        m.FolderPageModule)
  }
];
```

Think of a route as somewhat like a URL. The routing module defines an array of routes, and describes the pattern of URL to match, and describes which page modules get rendered for each.

The first route has an empty string for a path, with a redirectTo field. This means that there is no path specified, the application will default to folder/Inbox.

Next, any time the route starts with the word "folder/" followed by an ID, the application will import the folder module and follow that modules's own routing rules from there. I promise this will start to make sense as you build our own app.

folder.page.ts

Now you can look at something a little more interesting. Open src/app/folder/folder.page.ts, which defines the folder page component. There is not a lot of code in it.

```
@Component({
  selector: 'app-folder',
  templateUrl: './folder.page.html',
  styleUrls: ['./folder.page.scss'],
})
export class FolderPage implements OnInit {
  public folder: string;

  constructor(private activatedRoute: ActivatedRoute) { }

  ngOnInit() {
    this.folder = this
      .activatedRoute.snapshot.paramMap.get('id');
  }

}
```

It has a constructor, in which is injected an ActivatedRoute service. This is an angular service that lets you get information about the route the caused this page to appear. In the ngOnInit function, the page uses that service to get the id that was part of the route.

folder.page.html

The real magic happens in the folder page's markup, which is at src/app/folder/folder.page.html.

```html
<ion-header [translucent]="true">
  <ion-toolbar>
    <ion-buttons slot="start">
      <ion-menu-button></ion-menu-button>
    </ion-buttons>
    <ion-title>{{ folder }}</ion-title>
  </ion-toolbar>
</ion-header>

<ion-content [fullscreen]="true">
  <ion-header collapse="condense">
    <ion-toolbar>
      <ion-title size="large">{{ folder }}</ion-title>
    </ion-toolbar>
  </ion-header>

  <div id="container">
    <strong class="capitalize">{{ folder }}</strong>
    <p>Explore <a target="_blank" rel="noopener
noreferrer"
href="https://ionicframework.com/docs/components">UI
Components</a></p>
  </div>
</ion-content>
```

Most Ionic pages will contain an ion-header tag, which defines that fixed header at the top of the page. Inside of that is an ion-toolbar, a container for buttons, menus, and titles. To add buttons to a toolbar, you use an ion-buttons tag. The slot attribute indicates where in the header the buttons will go. The value "start" indicates that the buttons should be on the left on a left-to-right OS. You can also choose "end," which places the buttons on the right. Inside is a single button. The ion-menu-button is the standard hamburger menu you are all familiar with. By default, it shows and hides itself, but that can be overridden.

Next to the buttons is an ion-title, with the word folder surrounded by {{}}. You should now recognize this as an angular binding expression, telling Angular to replace that expression with the actual value of the folder variable.

Next is the ion-content. This is where most of your page's content will live. It contains another header and toolbar containing just a title.

Finally, you see an HTML div tag with another binding expression, and a paragraph containing a hyperlink.

Unbelievably, that is a good chunk of the functionality. Sure, there a bunch of other files, but these are the ones you need to be familiar with at this stage. The rest will be described as needed.

Now before you leave this little tour, I want to do a couple of fun things, but I will leave that for the next chapter.

Customize the Code

Before you leave this hello-ionic app, I want to do a couple of fun things. How do you think you might customize that page list? If you said, "modify the appPages array in app.component.ts," give yourself a pat on the back. I noticed that there is no Sent Mail page, so you will create one really quick and see what happens.

Put it right between Outbox and Favorites. Highlight the Outbox object, and press Option (or Alt if you are not on a Mac) and press the down arrow. This will make a copy of entire block of code. Change the second instance of the word Outbox to Sent Items, and the url to /folder/Sent. Leave the icon alone. Microsoft Outlook uses that paper airplane icon for sent items. So instead, change the icon for outbox to albums.

```
{
  title: 'Outbox',
  url: '/folder/Outbox',
  icon: 'albums'
},
{
  title: 'Sent Items',
  url: '/folder/Sent',
  icon: 'paper-plane'
},
```

Here is where it gets fun. Assuming you left the ionic serve command running, then as soon as you save these changes, the application will be rebuilt automatically, and the browser will reload to reflect these changes.

If not, run ionic serve again to see the changes.

Inbox
hi@ionicframework.com

✉	Inbox
📁	Outbox
✈	Sent Items
♥	Favorites
📥	Archived
🗑	Trash

What do you think will happen if you now click on the new Sent menu? You did not create a new page or route, so will you get a 404? Nope, the folder component will render, with its name set to the id portion of the route, which is Sent. This is because the folder component is a pretty generic object.

Not every page will be that clean, of course, but it is a good idea to look for places you can reuse this pattern.

If you want to see where those icons came from visit https://ionicons.com.

For more information on the components, you can click the components link right in the middle of the hello-ionic app itself.

And that wraps up this section. You should have a completely installed Ionic development environment, know how to create a new Ionic-Angular app, and even do some minor customizations.

So, go forth, delight in your newfound power. Play around a bit before you start the next chapter. When you are ready, I hope you will continue this journey with me.

A10Dance - The Demo App

The application you will be building throughout the course is called A10Dance. It is an attendance application originally designed to help Sunday School teachers keep track of the students in their classes.

For this book, the app will consist of three pages:

- A home page
- A Student Roster page
- A Student Detail page

A side menu will enable users easily navigate between the home and student roster pages. You will review how the menu is built, and navigation is configured to move from page to page.

The home page is where the application will start. There is not much here but an ion-card component. I will use this component to display some text information about the application.

The Roster page displays the students registered to the class and has most of the Ionic components you will use. The students are collectively displayed using an ion-list, with each list item consisting of ion-items, ion-buttons, ion-icons, and more. You will spend most of our time in the section covering this page, as you flesh out its functionality with action sheets, alerts, and toast notifications.

Finally, the Student detail page is where you can view and edit various details about a single student. You will eventually use this page to discuss Ionic forms. In this chapter, all you will do is lay out the components and bind some data to them.

At each step of the way, I will explain the components I have selected, and then provide the code that implements them.

Creating the New Project

Now that you have seen what you are going to build, dive right in and get the project up and running.

As I said earlier, before I start any new Ionic project, I want to make sure I am on the latest Ionic CLI. Do that first.

Run these commands

```
npm install -g @ionic/cli@latest
ionic start
```

When asked, select Angular as the framework. Next, supply the name of the project. I chose "a10dance." Select the blank template for this one. You will be implementing a side menu, but I would rather have us build it from scratch. Besides, this way you will be cutting a lot less boilerplate code.

If you are asked about Capacitor integration, say no. If it does not ask, but enables it automatically, that is fine.

You will not be working with AppFlow, so answer no to the question about connecting it to an Ionic account.

Once the project is created, you can open it in the IDE to have a look. There is not much there, because you used the blank template. That is OK, because you will build it up quickly.

Go back into the terminal and fire up a quick command:

```
ionic serve
```

Take a look at how it renders.

Again, there is not much content to speak of. So, take care of that next.

Modifying the Home Page

The first thing I want to do is flesh out the home page, as it is the app's landing page. There will not be much content – just some text inside an ion-card.

ion-card

An ion-card is a component designed to wrap basic pieces of information. By default, a card has a gray border, rounded edges, and a subtle drop shadow. As with all Ionic components, its visual style will change slightly when rendered on an Android versus an iPhone.

Cards can be as simple or as complex as you want. The card I envision for the home page will consist of an image of a classroom, followed by a card header having both a subtitle and title, and finally a brief intro paragraph inside of an ion-content tag.

You can get that page built right now.

Here is an image I will be using on the home page. It is available from the GitHub repo at https://github.com/walkingriver/at10dance-angular/raw/volume1-demo/src/assets/images/classroom.jpg.

Download that image now, or choose one of your own, and drop it into a new folder, src/assets/images. Call it classroom.jpg.

Open the home page, which is at src/app/home/home.page.html. Delete everything inside the <ion-content> tag.

Change the value inside the ion-title tag from Blank to Home.

In the now-empty ion-content, add an ion-card component.

Inside the ion-card, add a standard HTML <img> tag with the src attribute set to that file you just downloaded, which should be assets/images/classroom.jpg. To be a good citizen, you should also provide an alt attribute. I am using the word "Classroom".

Here is what the markup should look like at this point.

```
<ion-content>
  <ion-card>
    <img src="assets/images/classroom.jpg"
  </ion-card>
</ion-content>
```

Pause here, save the file, and see what it looks like. Then you can take advantage of live reloading as you finish the page.

VS Code Terminal

I want to show you a really cool feature of VS code, assuming you are using it. If not, enter the commands in whatever terminal you prefer. VS Code has a built-in terminal, which you can access by pressing Ctrl+`.

Inside the terminal, enter the command

```
npm start
```

You could also use ionic serve, but I want you to become accustomed to using npm as your script runner. It does not matter so much now, but you will eventually rely on npm to do more complex tasks for us. So, why not start now?

If all went well, you should see something like this.

Back in the code, add an ion-card-header component. By itself, that will not do much. So, inside that, add an ion-card-subtitle with the text "Classroom Attendance Manager," and immediately after it, an ion-card-title with the text "@10Dance." No, you do not have to spell it in the silly way I have.

Save the file and make sure it renders. If it did not, make sure the ion-card-header wraps the subtitle and title elements, and look for unclosed tags.

After the ion-card-header's closing tag, add an ion-card-content tag, and inside that a normal HTML paragraph tag. Put anything you want in that tag.

The component should now look like something this:

```
<ion-content>
  <ion-card>
    <img src="assets/images/classroom.jpg"
        alt="Classroom">
    <ion-card-header>
      <ion-card-subtitle>
        Classroom Attendance Manager</ion-card-subtitle>
      <ion-card-title>@10Dance</ion-card-title>
    </ion-card-header>
    <ion-card-content>
      <p>
      @10Dance is an attendance application originally
designed to help Sunday School teachers keep track of the
students in their classes.
      </p>
    </ion-card-content>
  </ion-card>
</ion-content>
```

Save the file and check the results. It should mostly resemble what I have here.

Now do one more thing before you leave the Home page. Put in a link to the Roster page, which you will build shortly.

After the paragraph tag, add an HTML anchor tag with two attributes: a routerLink set to "/roster" and a routerDirection set to "forward." Inside the tag provide some text, such as "go to roster." This will create a button with declarative navigation, so that you can go to the roster page once it exists.

The reason you use routerLink instead of the typical href attribute is so that Ionic will enhance the navigation animation for you. The routerDirection means to use the platforms typical forward animation direction. You could also have specified back or root, which have slightly different animations.

It should now look like this:

```
<ion-card-content>
  <p>
    @10Dance is an attendance application originally
    designed to help Sunday School teachers keep
    track of the students in their classes.
  </p>
</ion-card-content>
```

Saving the page, you can see the link rendered. However, clicking on it will take you to a blank page. You have not built the Roster page yet. You will do that shortly.

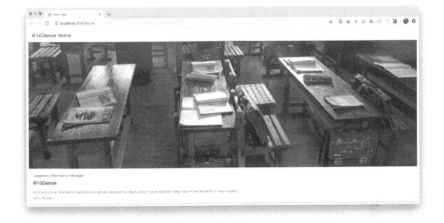

Custom Students Service

Before you flesh out the Roster page, you need to get some students to display. Later you will want to tie the list into a data store of some sort, but you do not need to do that just to get some data displayed on the page.

For that, you are going to create a simple "Students" service you can inject into the pages that need it. Use the command line to create the service.

Angular CLI

In this case, it does not matter whether or not you use the Angular CLI or the Ionic CLI. Go ahead and use the Angular CLI this time. Enter the following command.

```
npx ng generate service Students --dry-run
```

In case this is your first time seeing npx, I will explain. When you install npm packages globally, as you did with the Ionic CLI, the package's main binary will be linked to a folder that is already in your execution path.

On the other hand, the Ionic-Angular project template installs the Angular CLI as a local project dependency. This means that the entire Angular CLI is installed in your project's node_modules folder. This makes is visible to your project's npm scripts, but completely invisible to your system. When you type ng into your terminal, it has no idea where to find that command.

The npx command, which is installed with node and npm, knows to look for commands inside of your node_modules command.

This command is simply instructing the Angular CLI to generate a service named Students. The dry-run option gives you a chance to see what will happen, and then tweak things if you do not like what you see.

```
CREATE src/app/students.service.spec.ts (338 bytes)
CREATE src/app/students.service.ts (136 bytes)
NOTE: The "dryRun" flag means no changes were made.
```

By default, the service will be created in the app folder, but not in a folder of its own, and it will be created with a unit test. Go ahead and run it again without the dry-run flag. When it has finished, open students.service.ts.

Inside this file you will create an interface, a constant, and a function.

Create a Student object as an interface. Remember, interfaces do not exist in JavaScript, and will completely vanish upon build. Their sole purpose for us is to enable parameter type checking, code completion, and intellisense inside the code editor.

```
export interface Student {
  id: string;
  firstName: string;
  lastName: string;
  birthDate?: string;
  parentName?: string;
  parentEmail?: string;
  parentPhone?: string;
  photoUrl?: string;
```

```
    status?: 'present' | 'absent';
}
```

The question marks on most of the fields indicate that those fields are optional. To create a valid Student object, you need to provide at least an id, firstName, and lastName. At this point, I do not know everything that a Student object should have, but these fields should be enough for our purposes now.

The status is worth noting due to its odd type. TypeScript allows you to specify what essentially becomes a compile-time validation check.

```
    status?: 'present' | 'absent';
```

This line indicates that the status field is an optional string value, which may only contain one of two values: present or absent. Though this will not be enforced at runtime, the TypeScript compiler will prevent you from assigning any other value, and VS Code will offer you smart code completion when assigning a value to this field.

Next, create an array of students that you can use in place of a database for now. Call it mockStudents.

```
const mockStudents: Student[] = [
    { id: '1', firstName: 'Greg', lastName: 'Marine' },
    { id: '2', firstName: 'Jonathan', lastName: 'Bennett' },
    { id: '3', firstName: 'Neil', lastName: 'Estandarte' },
    { id: '4', firstName: 'Jen', lastName: 'Townsend' },
    { id: '5', firstName: 'Casey', lastName: 'McBride' },
    { id: '6', firstName: 'Diane', lastName: 'Rivera' },
    { id: '7', firstName: 'Troy', lastName: 'Gutierrez' },
    { id: '8', firstName: 'Priscilla', lastName: 'Little' },
    { id: '9', firstName: 'Bobby', lastName: 'Robbins' },
    { id: '10', firstName: 'Edmund', lastName: 'Gardner' }
]
```

Now for the function. Create a function called getAll(). This will return a copy of the mockStudents array. In a future volume, you will flesh out this service with more functionality, but for now, this is plenty.

```
getAll() {
   return [...mockStudents];
}
```

If you have not seen that particular syntax, it is shorthand for making a shallow copy of an array.

When you are finished, the complete StudentsService class should look something like this.

```
@Injectable({
   providedIn: 'root'
})
export class StudentsService {

   constructor() { }

   getAll() {
      return [...mockStudents];
   }
}
```

It is deceptively simple because it does not do much. Now go create that Roster Page.

Adding the Roster Page

By now, you should be comfortable adding Ionic tags into a page, but you have not created a new page from scratch yet. You will tackle that now, by creating what will arguably be the most complicated page in the application.

To create a new Ionic page, you can use either the Ionic CLI or the Angular CLI. One of the things I like best about using Angular with Ionic is the rich templating that Angular brings to the table.

Ionic delegates much of its command line operations to the underlying Angular CLI, augmenting it where appropriate. Creating pages is one of these appropriate times. Angular has no default scaffolding for creating pages, only components. While a page is implemented as an Angular component, Ionic provides you with a slightly richer experience with their Page scaffolding. The really wonderful thing is that this scaffolding can be used by either the Ionic or the Angular CLI. It is up to you which you want to use.

In the terminal, enter either of these commands. They will do the same thing.

```
ionic generate page Roster --dry-run
npx ng generate page Roster --dry-run
```

Again, I recommend using the dry-run option to see what it will do ahead of time. Also note that you will not need to use npx with the ionic command, because the Ionic CLI is installed globally.

The command output will look something like this.

```
CREATE src/app/roster/roster-routing.module.ts (351 bytes)
CREATE src/app/roster/roster.module.ts (479 bytes)
CREATE src/app/roster/roster.page.scss (0 bytes)
```

```
CREATE src/app/roster/roster.page.html (126 bytes)
CREATE src/app/roster/roster.page.spec.ts (654 bytes)
CREATE src/app/roster/roster.page.ts (260 bytes)
UPDATE src/app/app-routing.module.ts (869 bytes)

NOTE: The "dryRun" flag means no changes were made.
```

The output indicates that the generate command will create a new roster folder, a page, a separate module for the page, tests, and styles. Plus, it will automatically add the page into the app's routing system. See? Much of the grunt work is done for you.

Go ahead and rerun the same command, without the dry-run option.

Save everything. If the npm start command is still running, everything should rebuild and re-render. If not, go ahead and run the command again from the terminal.

```
npm start
```

Once it finishes building, you can re-render your home page. Click the Roster link. The default roster page just created will be displayed. There is not much there, but you will take care of that in the next chapter.

Implementing a Student Roster

Now you need to put those students you just created into the roster page. Open src/app/roster/roster.page.ts.

Just before the constructor, create an array of students to hold the list you will retrieve from the StudentsService:

```
//This will hold the list of students
students: Student[] = [];
```

Next, you need to inject a reference to the StudentsService into the page's constructor. Insert a new private parameter studentService, of type StudentsService.

```
constructor(
  private studentService: StudentsService) { }
```

Make sure you get the casing right, or Angular will not be happy with you. Marking the parameter private automatically exposes the parameter as a member of the component class. It is a handy shortcut TypeScript provides.

By default, the RosterPage implements Angular's OnInit interface, which requires you to implement the OnInit Angular hook you saw in the guided tour.

The function implementation, called ngOnInit, should currently be empty. Inside this function, call the getAllStudents function from the StudentService, and assign its result to the component's students array.

```
ngOnInit() {
  this.students = this.studentService.getAll();
}
```

Now open the roster.page.html file in the same folder, so you can create some markup to render the students.

The header is already done, and its name should be set to Roster, so there is nothing you need to do there. You could change it to "Class Roster" or something if you really want.

I am hoping that the ion-header is familiar, as you have seen it on the home page, and during the guided tour.

Immediately after the ion-header, you need an ion-content. Inside the ion-content, I will introduce a new component: The ion-list.

ion-list

An ion-list is another container component, designed to wrap multiple types of items in a visually consistent manner. ion-lists contain things called ion-items, which in turn wrap ion-labels, ion-buttons, ion-icons, form input fields and so forth. You will use all of those and more during this book.

ion-lists can also be used to implement item sliding, which you have probably seen before. These are options that appear only when you swipe a list item left or right, revealing a less often used, or potentially dangerous option, such as delete.

Inside of the ion-list, you can iterate over the students array with an *ngFor directive on the outermost element inside the list. In this case, it will be an ion-item-sliding component. It will look like this.

```
<ion-item-sliding *ngFor="let student of students">
```

This will create one ion-item-sliding component (and everything inside it) for each student in the students array.

ion-item-sliding will provide us with the item swipe, or slide, option. Inside that will be an ion-item tag. This component will encapsulate the complete list item.

Inside the ion-item, add an ion-icon and an ion-label as siblings. Set the icon's slot attribute to "start," meaning that it will appear at the start of the line. Inside the ion-label, bind some text to the student's last and first names, separated by a comma.

Next to those, create two more ion-icon tags, which you will conditionally render based on the student's status of absent or present. The first one is for present; set it to display the eye icon. The second is to be displayed when the student is absent, so for that one, use the eye-off-outline, which is an outline of an eye with a line through it.

The way you render the icons conditionally is to add the *ngIf directive to each icon. One will evaluate to true if the student's status is present. The other will render if the student's status is absent.

Note that it is entirely possible for the student's status to be set to neither value, because the status field is optional. In that case, neither icon will be rendered, which is what I want.

Here is the completed ion-content code with the list.

```
<ion-content>
  <ion-list>
    <ion-item-sliding *ngFor="let student of students">
      <ion-item>
        <ion-icon slot="start" name="person-outline">
        </ion-icon>
        <ion-label>
          {{student.lastName}}, {{student.firstName}}
        </ion-label>
        <ion-icon *ngIf="student.status==='present'"
          slot="end" name="eye"></ion-icon>
        <ion-icon *ngIf="student.status==='absent'"
          slot="end" name="eye-off-outline">
        </ion-icon>
      </ion-item>
    </ion-item-sliding>
  </ion-list>
```

```
</ion-content>
```

Save the file now and see how it looks. If all went well, all of our students are displayed as expected.

I want to wrap up this chapter by finishing that sliding item. Immediately before the ion-itemSliding closing tag, add an ion-itemOptions slide, with the side attribute set to end. This means you want the option to appear at the end of the item, meaning when you slide it toward the beginning of the item.

Inside of that tag, add a single ion-itemOption tag (mind the singular/plural here. The plural tag is the outer tag). Set this one's color to danger, which by default is a scary looking orange/red color. You will deal with the click handler later, so for now, simply set the tag's value to the word Delete. The complete code should now look like this.

```
<ion-content>
  <ion-list>
    <ion-item-sliding *ngFor="let student of students">
      <ion-item>
        <ion-icon slot="start" name="person-outline">
        </ion-icon>
```

```
          <ion-label>
            {{student.lastName}}, {{student.firstName}}
          </ion-label>
          <ion-icon *ngIf="student.status==='present'"
            slot="end" name="eye"></ion-icon>
          <ion-icon *ngIf="student.status==='absent'"
            slot="end" name="eye-off-outline"></ion-icon>
        </ion-item>
        <ion-item-options side="end">
          <ion-item-option color="danger">Delete
          </ion-item-option>
        </ion-item-options>
      </ion-item-sliding>
    </ion-list>
</ion-content>
```

Save the file and refresh the page. At this point, the only interactivity is the slider itself, so click and drag an item towards the beginning of the item. You should see a Delete button. You can click it. It behaves visually as you would expect it to, but it will not do anything…yet.

In the next chapter you will wire up some new commands to this page so that you can manage our roster of students.

Adding Functionality to the Student Roster

If you were a teacher and this were a real class of students, there are a number of things you would want to be able to do with your app. A few of those things are:

- Mark Absent or Present.
- Navigate to a detail page to see or edit information that is not present on the list.
- Remove a student from the class, with the appropriate warnings, of course.

In this chapter, you will enhance the UI of the Roster page to do all of these things.

The first thing I want to do is add a menu to each student in the ion-list. You can either create the menu first or the button to launch the menu first. Go and create the menu first. For that, you are going to use an ion-action-sheet.

ion-action-sheet

An action sheet is a menu that displays like a dialog. It often contains at least two, but usually more, action buttons that are contextually related in some way. In our case, the context is that of the currently selected student.

An ion-action-sheet is Ionic's specific implementation, rendering an action sheet that automatically looks at home on an iPhone or Android.

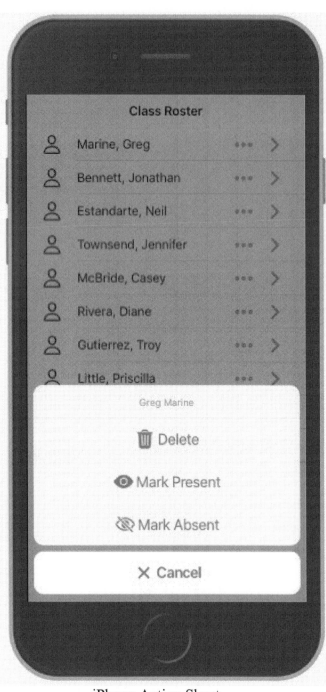

iPhone Action Sheet

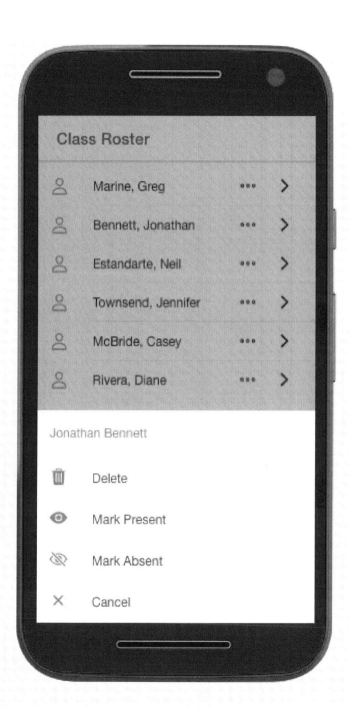

Android Action Sheet

Buttons in an action sheet may contain a role, which can be either destructive or cancel. Destructive is used to indicate that something permanent can happen and is often used for delete operations. On iOS devices, buttons with the destructive role are rendered differently than the rest, usually in red.

A button whose role is cancel will always be rendered last, at the bottom of the sheet. This button should have no purpose other than dismissing the sheet with no action taken.

The buttons in an action sheet can have text and icons. However, the way you define them is unlike a normal ion-button component.

Our action sheet will include buttons to mark a student as present or absent, delete a student, or cancel the action and do nothing. In order to do that, you need to do a bit of setup first.

In the roster.page.ts file, you need to inject the ActionSheetController into the component's constructor. This will enable us to build an action sheet in response to a button click. The updated constructor should now look like this.

```
constructor(
    private actionSheetController: ActionSheetController,
    private studentService: StudentsService) { }
```

Yes, I like keeping my constructor parameters in alphabetical order, but it is not necessary. Ensure you import ActionSheetController from '@ionic/angular' if VS Code does not do it for you.

Now create a function to delete a student.

```
async deleteStudent(student: Student) {
    this.students = this.students
      .filter(x => x.id !== student.id);
}
```

This function works by calling the filter function on the students array, removing the student passed into the function, and then reassigning the result of the filter to the students array.

Now create the action sheet. The function to create and present the action sheet looks like this.

```
async presentActionSheet(student: Student) {
    const actionSheet = await this.actionSheetController
    .create({
      header: `${student.firstName} ${student.lastName}`,

      await actionSheet.present();
}
```

The create function accepts an options object and returns a promise, which resolves to the action sheet component itself. This means you must await it, which means the function has to be marked as async.

At a minimum, you will want to provide a header and an array of buttons. The code above sets the header to the concatenation of the provided student's first and last names.

Once you have a reference to the action sheet component, you can display by calling its present function. This function also returns a promise, so you may wish to await that call also.

Continuing with the options object, you need to create the buttons array. This is an array of button objects. Each button should have a text field and an icon field, a handler function that gets called when a user clicks it, and optionally a role value. For this action sheet, create four buttons:

1. Delete, with the role of destructive, the trash icon, and a handler function which calls deleteStudent.
2. Mark Present, with the eye icon, and a handler function which sets the selected student's status to Present.

3. Mark Absent, with the eye-off-outline icon, and a handler function which sets the selected student's status to Absent.
4. And finally, a cancel button with the close icon and the role of cancel. It does not need a handler.

Below is entire code for the action sheet.

```
async presentActionSheet(student: Student) {
  const actionSheet = await this.actionSheetController
  .create({
    header: `${student.firstName} ${student.lastName}`,
    buttons: [{
      text: 'Mark Present',
      icon: 'eye',
      handler: () => {
        this.markPresent(student);
      }
    }, {
      text: 'Mark Absent',
      icon: 'eye-off-outline',
      handler: () => {
        student.status = 'present';
      }
    }, {
      text: 'Delete',
      icon: 'trash',
      role: 'destructive',
      handler: () => {
        this.deleteStudent(student);
      }
    }, {
      text: 'Cancel',
      icon: 'close',
      role: 'cancel',
      handler: () => {
        console.log('Cancel clicked');
      }
    }]
  });

  await actionSheet.present();
}
```

Now create a button to launch the action sheet. Open the roster page markup and add an ion-buttons tag immediately after the two existing icons, and right before the ion-item closing tag. Give it a slot attribute set to end, meaning that it will appear at the end of the item. Next, add two ion-button tags, as children of the ion-buttons tag. Inside of each button, add an ion-icon with a slot attribute set to icon-only. This will suppress space in the button for a text label. Specify the name of the first as ellipsis-horizontal-outline and set the second one to chevron-forward-outline. These names map to the name of the icons from https://ionicons.com.

Add a click handler to the button with the ellipsis. When clicked, you want to call the presentActionSheet function, passing the current student from the array.

Leave the button with the chevron alone for now. You will finish that one later.

When you are finished, your ion-buttons component should look something like this.

```
<ion-buttons slot="end">
  <ion-button (click)="presentActionSheet(student)">
    <ion-icon slot="icon-only"
              name="ellipsis-horizontal-outline">
    </ion-icon>
  </ion-button>
  <ion-button>
    <ion-icon slot="icon-only"
              name="chevron-forward-outline"></ion-icon>
  </ion-button>
</ion-buttons>
```

Save the file and have a look at the results. Click the buttons and see that they look and behave as you would expect. The forward caret will not do anything, but the ellipsis icon should display a completely functional action sheet.

You should be able to mark students present or absent, and see the icon change accordingly. Likewise, you can also delete a student.

Connect Sliding Delete Button

While you are here, you can wire up the Delete button in the ion-item-option component. Simply add a click handler and call deleteStudent.

```
<ion-item-option (click)="deleteStudent(student)">
  color="danger" Delete</ion-item-option>
```

ion-buttons and icons

You may be wondering, what is an ion-buttons tag, and why can you not simply drop a button where you want it? While buttons can generally be placed anywhere you want them, when used inside an ion-item or ion-toolbar component, you need to group them together inside an ion-buttons tag, specifying the slot as start or end, depending on where you want the buttons to display. As with everything else in Ionic, start typically places the buttons on the left side of its parent component, and end places them on the right. This order is reversed for locales that traditionally read Right-to-Left.

The ion-button component itself acts as you expect and can be customized in a variety of ways. Buttons can be text-only, icon-only, or a combination of the two. Buttons can be rendered large or small, in multiple widths, and in a variety of colors. When adding an icon to a button, specify the icon's slot as start or end, depending on whether you want the icon to appear before or after the button's text. To create a button without any text, specify the slot as icon-only and do not include any text.

As stated above, all the Ionic icons can be found at https://ionicons.com.

User Confirmation and Notification

The way the code is currently written, deleting a student from the roster might be done accidentally if the user clicks or taps on the wrong button in the action sheet. There is no warning or confirmation requested. Likewise, when a student is deleted, there is no indication that the action occurred (other than the name disappearing from the list). You will address both of these shortcomings in this chapter.

Delete Confirmation

It is inconsiderate for an app to take a destructive action without at least warning the user. It is better to ask for confirmation, and that is what you will do here. In the previous chapter, both of the Delete buttons simply call the deleteStudent function. Instead, it would be better to get a confirmation first. You can get that confirmation using an ion-alert.

ion-alert

An ion-alert is a modal UI component that provides a simple warning to the user that something important is about to happen, and optionally provide a way to cancel it.

Below is what I have in mind to implement the confirmation. As with all Ionic components, it renders with the appropriate look and feel on both Android and iPhone.

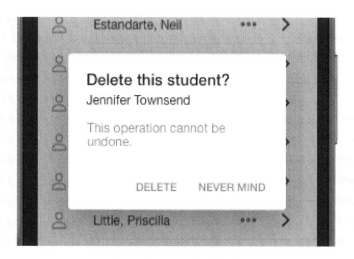

ion-alert on Android

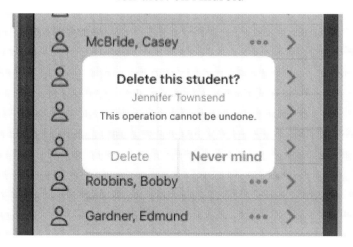

ion-alert on iPhone

Implementing an ion-alert on the Roster page will closely resemble the work done on the ion-action-sheet, and with good reason. Ionic has tried to keep the development experience consistent. Much of the following code should feel familiar.

Inside the Roster page's component code, you need to inject Ionic's AlertController into the constructor. Make sure it gets imported at the top of the file.

```
constructor(
  private actionSheetController: ActionSheetController,
  private alertController: AlertController,
  private studentService: StudentsService
) { }
```

Next, create a new function called presentDeleteAlert. In the markup where you are currently calling deleteStudent, change that to call presentDeleteAlert.

```
async presentDeleteAlert(student: Student) {
  const alert = await this.alertController.create(
    {
      header: 'Delete this student?',
      subHeader:
        `${student.firstName} ${student.lastName}`,
      message: 'This operation cannot be undone.',
      buttons: [
        {
          text: 'Delete',
          handler: () => this.deleteStudent(student)
        },
        {
          text: 'Never mind',
          role: 'cancel'
        }
      ]
    }
  );

  await alert.present();
}
```

There are three attributes that control the text inside an ion-alert.

The header attribute is a string that appears at the top of the alert. Use something like "Delete this student?" The subHeader attribute appears just inside the alert body. Set this attribute to a concatenation of the student's first and last names, so the user knows for sure exactly which student is about to be deleted. The message attribute is the main body of the alert. Use a string such as, "This operation cannot be undone."

Finally, the alert needs an array of buttons. You define these buttons exactly the same way as you did for the action sheet.

The first button is the Delete button. It needs a handler that will delete a student, so provide an arrow function that simply calls the presentDeleteAlert function.

The second button should be a Cancel button, with the role of "cancel." It does not need a handler.

Save and check your work. If all went well, attempting to delete a student should no longer automatically work. Instead, you should now see the alert asking for confirmation. Clicking the button with the role set to "cancel" should dismiss the alert with no action taken. Only if you select the Delete button will the student disappear.

Next, you will create a small acknowledgement to the user that the student really was deleted.

Toast Notifications

Many times, an application needs to provide a notification to the user that something has happened, but it is not critical enough to interrupt the flow of the application completely. Toast notifications fill that role perfectly.

A toast is a small, unobtrusive pop-up informational banner. By convention, it should impart a short message that will appear for a brief amount of time before automatically disappearing. Some toast notifications also contain a way for the user to dismiss it early.

Deciding whether or not to use a toast notification is simple. Does the message require the user to take action? And is it important if the user misses it? If the answer to both questions is "no," then a toast notification is perfect.

ion-toast

The Ionic implementation of a toast notification is the ion-toast component. It is probably the most basic of all of Ionic's UI components. You can build one with a minimal amount of effort. The most basic form of the component consists of a message and a

duration.

An ion-toast can be vertically positioned at the top, middle, or bottom of the screen. It is always centered horizontally. It can be colored with the "color" attribute, providing any of the Ionic color constants. You can add buttons and icons.

You will not be doing any of that. If you want to customize your ion-toast after you finish the chapter, feel free.

Implementing the ion-toast

In the roster page's component, add Ionic's ToastController to the constructor.

```
constructor(
  private actionSheetController: ActionSheetController,
  private alertController: AlertController,
  private studentService: StudentsService,
  private toastController: ToastController) { }
```

Next, modify the deleteStudent function to create and immediately present a toast notification. My version now looks like this.

```
async deleteStudent(student: Student) {
  this.students = this.students
    .filter(x => x.id !== student.id);

  const alert = await this.toastController.create(
    {
      message:
      `${student.firstName} ${student.lastName} deleted.`,
      position: 'top',
      duration: 3000
    });

  await alert.present();
}
```

Its message attribute should contain a short statement showing that the student has been deleted. Be as detailed as you want but remember that shorter is usually better.

The default toast position is vertically centered on the screen. I decided to move it to the top but will leave the final decision to you. You can choose from top, middle, or bottom.

The duration attribute controls how long the ion-toast will wait before it automatically dismisses itself. The duration is an integer in milliseconds. Be careful not to specify a duration that is too short, and definitely do not pass a string. If you omit the duration attribute, the toast will remain on the screen indefinitely, requiring user intervention to dismiss it.

You can provide a buttons array to an ion-toast, just as with the ion-action-sheet and ion-alert. If you feel so inclined, go ahead and add one.

Save the file and let the browser refresh.

Now when you delete a student, in addition to the student's name disappearing from the roster, you should also see the confirmation toast.

If you want some ideas on how to improve this experience, I provide some in the Challenges section later in the book.

Basic Navigation Menu

Before you wrap up this volume, I want to add a menu to make it easier to navigate between the home page and the roster page. The menu will mostly look and act like the one from the guided tour, but it will be a bit simpler. In Ionic, you create a menu with the ion-menu component.

ion-menu

The ion-menu is the Ionic component that implements a side-menu. As with most other Ionic container components, it can contain a header with a toolbar and title, along with some ion-content. The typical side-menu consists of a list of options, made from an ion-list of ion-items.

The menu can be customized with a variety of behaviors.

If you want the menu to obscure the main page content when it opens, you can set its type attribute to overlay. With this option, the menu slides in from the side, covering the stationary main content.

Another option is push, which causes the page content to slide with the menu. The menu still slides in from the side, pushing the main content out of the way.

Or you can choose reveal to achieve a similar, but subtly different effect from overlay. With reveal, the menu content itself is stationary, and appears to be uncovered as the main contents slides out of the way.

You can specify which side the menu is on by setting the side attribute to either start or end. If you choose end, make sure your menu icon is on the same side of the main content's toolbar, or it will look weird.

You can disable swiping the menu on mobile devices by setting swipeGesture to false.

If you want an item in your menu to close the menu when you select it, be sure to wrap it with an ion-menu-toggle component. Otherwise, the menu will stay open.

The ion-menu-toggle can also be used to open a menu (hence the name toggle). By default, it will automatically hide itself whenever it detects that its menu is disabled or being presented in a split-pane, as you will be doing here. Because of that, if you want it to be visible all the time, be sure to set its autoHide attribute to false.

Do not ask me how long it took me to debug that the first time I forgot it.

Below are examples of the three different menu types.

There is more to the menu, but those are the basics. You will build one in the next section.

ion-menu "overlay" type

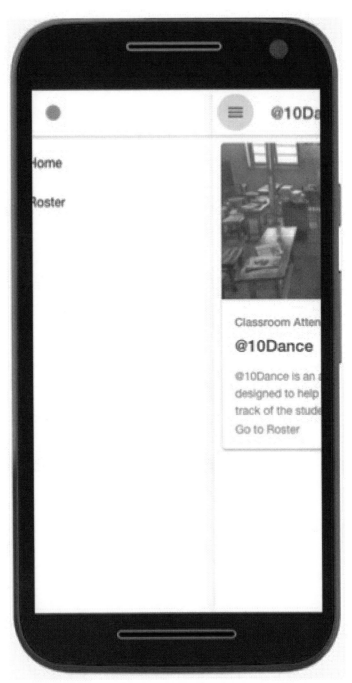

ion-menu "push" Type

ion-menu "reveal" Type

Menu Implementation

Open the file src/app/app.component.ts. This is where you will define the menu.

Replicating what you saw during the tour, create an array of pages. Inside the array, provide two object literals: one for the home page, with the appropriate url and icon; then one for the Roster page, with its URL /roster, and use the icon called people.

```
const appPages = [
  {
    title: 'Home',
    url: '/home',
    icon: home
  },
  {
    title: 'Roster',
    url: '/roster',
    icon: people
  }
];
```

Next comes the menu itself. That will live inside the app component markup, src/app/app.component.html, which should be pretty empty right now. You need to flesh it out by adding some Ionic components.

To build the menu content, create an ion-menu element as the first element inside of the ion-app element. Set its contentId to main-content. This value must match the HTML element id of the ion-router-outlet, so add an id attribute to ion-router-outlet with the same value.

For the menu type, I am partial to overlay, but feel free to try push or reveal.

Add an ion-header, with an ion-toolbar, and an ion-title. Inside the title, provide a title such as Menu.

This is what the markup should look like at this point.

```
<ion-app>
  <ion-menu contentId="main-content" type="overlay">
    <ion-header>
      <ion-toolbar>
        <ion-title>Menu</ion-title>
      </ion-toolbar>
    </ion-header>
  </ion-menu>
  <ion-router-outlet id="main-content">
  </ion-router-outlet>
</ion-app>
```

Just after the ion-header, add an ion-content. And just inside that an ion-list. This is where the menu will be constructed, by iterating over the appPages array.

As you did with the students, you will use an ngFor directive inside of an ion-menu-toggle component.

```
<ion-menu-toggle auto-hide="false" *ngFor="let p of appPages; let i = index">
```

This is a slightly different ngFor expression than you have seen previously. It is looping over the appPages array, but there is also the second portion, let i = index. This does what you probably suspect, providing an integer representing the array index of each page in the array.

As I mentioned earlier, set the auto-hide property to false, unless you enjoy watching things vanish for no apparent reason.

Inside the toggle, place an ion-item with a routerLink set to appPage.url. Doing this automatically turns the item into a hyperlink, which is pretty cool. Make sure you get the binding syntax right, as I am showing here. Otherwise, you could end up sending your users to a route literally called "appPage.url." Set the routerDirection to none or root, your choice. This affects the animation. It is subtle, so play with it and decide which you prefer.

Also include a click handler to the ion-item that sets selectedIndex = i. This allows the app component to track the current page. With a little CSS styling, it is reasonably simple to highlight that page in the menu.

You can do that by conditionally adding the selected class with the expression [class.selected]="selectedIndex == i". Recall that specifying an attribute inside of square brackets causes Angular to execute the expression in quotes on the right side of the = sign. If the expression evaluates to true, then the class will be applied. The only thing missing is the custom styling for the selected class, but I will leave that as an exercise for you.

If you want a visible line separating your menu items, set the lines attribute to "full" or omit the attribute entirely. I am not a fan of the looks, so I tend to choose "none."

Finally, set detail to false. That will prevent the menu from having a gray forward chevron on its side. I do not like the effect for a menu, but to each his own.

Inside the ion-item, add an ion-icon with its slot set to start and its name set to the page.icon. Again, pay attention to the binding syntax.

Your complete menu should look like this.

```
<ion-menu contentId="main-content" type="overlay">
  <ion-header>
    <ion-toolbar>
      <ion-title>Menu</ion-title>
    </ion-toolbar>
  </ion-header>
  <ion-content>
    <ion-list id="inbox-list">
      <ion-menu-toggle auto-hide="false"
```

```
      *ngFor="let page of appPages; let i = index">
      <ion-item (click)="selectedIndex = i"
        routerDirection="root"
        [routerLink]="[page.url]"
        lines="none"
        detail="false"
        [class.selected]="selectedIndex == i">
        <ion-icon slot="start" [name]="page.icon">
        </ion-icon>
        <ion-label>{{ page.title }}</ion-label>
      </ion-item>
    </ion-menu-toggle>
  </ion-list>
  </ion-content>
</ion-menu>
```

Make sure you close all your tags properly.

Menu Button

You need to add a menu icon to both of our pages. Nope, it is not automatic. Open src/app/home/home.page.html.

Inside the ion-toolbar, just before the ion-title, you need to add an ion-buttons component with slot="start". Then an ion-menu-button component inside of that.

You do not need to add any text or icons. Those will be managed automatically.

Then you need to do exactly the same code in the Roster page. Just copy and paste the same block of code.

Both page's headers should now look like this, with the appropriate value for ion-title, of course.

```
<ion-header>
  <ion-toolbar>
```

```
    <ion-buttons slot="start">
      <ion-menu-button></ion-menu-button>
    </ion-buttons>
    <ion-title>Home</ion-title>
  </ion-toolbar>
</ion-header>
```

Save the files and try it.

If all went well, you should now be able to navigate between the home and roster pages with ease.

Split Pane

The one thing left to do is to implement the split pane. Remember in the guided tour, you saw that when the window was narrow, as on a mobile device, the menu was hidden, and would slide out from the side when you click on the menu icon.

The split pane allows you to keep the menu visible when the screen is wide enough. Though you can override this behavior, as a general rule, "wide enough" means if the HTML page is wider than 992 pixels.

Adding the split pane requires just two more lines of code. Back in src/app/app.component.html, as the first child of ion-app, just before the ion-menu, add an ion-split-pane component with the contentId attribute set to main-content. Yes, this exactly matches the contentId attribute of the menu and the id attribute of the ion-router-outlet. This is how Ionic knows that the three components are tied together.

Should you want, you can add a when attribute to the ion-split-pane to indicate when you want it visible. Valid values are xs, sm, md, lg, or xl. The default is lg. Play around with them and choose the one you like best.

Wrap Up

To recap what just happened in this Chapter: if you want to add a page, these are the things you should do:

- Create the page component itself, with the markup and code you want.
- Add a route with a URL so that users can get to the page.
- If you want the page in your application's side menu, add it to the appPages array, with the URL, a title, and an icon.
- Repeat as needed.

There will be more pages in future volumes of this series. I hope you will join me.

Where to Go from Here?

I hope you enjoyed this introduction to developing web applications with Ionic and Angular. By this point, you should be comfortable with:

- The basics of the Ionic Framework.
- Some of the "Angularisms" and how they work with Ionic.
- Looking for more information in the Ionic Documentation.
- Building a functional UI composed of various Ionic Components.

This is Volume One in the series: *Ionic and Angular: Idea to App Store*. Please look for the other volumes in this series.

Ionic and Angular Video Course

I mentioned this before, but it bears repeating. There is also an online video version of this course, encompassing this entire book series.

More information on the courses, along with occasional discount codes, can be found by signing up on my website: https://walkingriver.com.

Reviews Appreciated!

If you enjoyed this book, please consider leaving me a review on Amazon and Goodreads .

Apply What You Have Learned

Now that you have completed this volume, take a few moments to apply what you have learned to the demo application you just built. Here are a few enhancements you attempt.

Modify the "Delete" Toast

The toast notification you added to indicate that a student was deleted from the roster positions itself at the top of the screen, stays for 3000 ms (3 seconds), and then vanishes. It cannot be manually dismissed by the user. And sometimes, it can be a little hard to see in its default color and position. Your challenge is to fix that.

1. Change the duration of the toast to 5 seconds.
2. Add a close button so the user can close the toast sooner. Toast buttons are configured the same way that Action Sheet buttons are. Hint: use a role rather than a handler.
3. Move the toast to the bottom or middle of the screen using its position attribute.
4. Change its color.

Modify the Icons

Maybe you do not like my icons. Head over to https://ionicons.com and find some you like better. Here are some ideas:

1. You can change the absent/present icons to something else, change their colors, or both.
2. The icon you use in the roster is pretty generic. You could add a gender to the Student interface and then adjust the icon based on that value at runtime.
3. Change the color of any icon.

Advanced: Undo Delete

Instead of a close button on the toast notification, you could add a quick "undo" button.

Advanced: Sort Roster

TypeScript arrays have a sort function. Provide a button in the Roster toolbar to sort by the students' last names instead of the current default.

Advanced: Header Component

It seems that every page needs a header with a title and menu button. For a demo application with only two pages, copying and pasting the header code might be acceptable. As your app grows, this might become a burden. Create a custom component that includes a menu button, with a title you can pass as an attribute.

References

https://ionicframework.com/docs

Appendix – Installing the Tools

Windows Quick Start

If you are on Windows, this section should get you up and running as quickly as possible. I am going to assume you do not have any of the following tools. If you do, please just skip that step.

Git

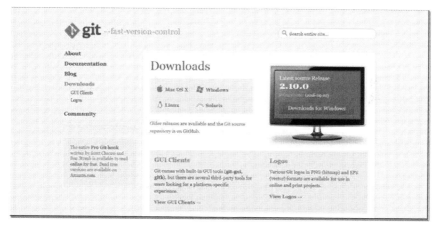

First, you will need the latest version of Git. Depending on your code editor or IDE of choice, it is possible to avoid typing most git commands.

Git for Windows installs an alternative command prompt, called Git Bash. I recommend using that over the windows command prompt wherever possible.

You should be able to click the Downloads for Windows button, select the default for your system (probably the 64-bit Git for Windows, and then install with the default options.

Node

Next, you will need to have NodeJS, which will become the foundation of everything you do in this book.

The most straightforward method is downloading and installing it right from nodejs.org. It is quick and painless. The only real drawback is that it limits you to only one version of Node being installed at a time. Unbelievably, that can be a real problem for some developers, who support multiple apps, each built on a different version of Node. It will not be a problem for this book, so you are safe in installing from here.

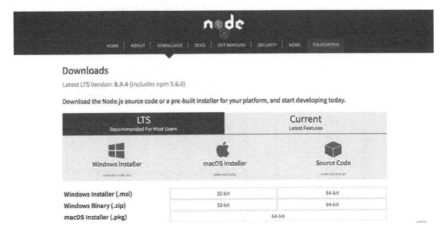

Visit https://nodejs.org. You will want to download the latest LTS (or long-term support) version of Node.

Once downloaded, simply run the installer. Accepting the installer's defaults should get you what you need.

macOS Quick Start

If you use a Mac, this section will show you how to install the tools you are going to need. If you are not using a Mac, feel free to skip ahead to the next section.

Homebrew

On a Mac, most of the tools you need to install can be installed through Homebrew. Homebrew bills itself as the Mac's missing package manager.

There are a lot of tools and runtime packages available through Homebrew, so I recommend installing it if you do not already have it. You can install it by copying and pasting the following command into any terminal window.

```
/bin/bash -c "$(curl -fsSL
https://raw.githubusercontent.com/Homebrew/install/master/
install.sh)"
```

Git

Next you should install Git. But first, check to see if you have it. In a terminal window, enter the command

```
git --version
```

If it is installed, you will see a version number, probably 2.x or something. If you have a version that says, "Apple Git," it means you installed it through the XCode command line tools. This should be ok.

If you do not have git, and you installed Homebrew, simply issue the command

```
brew install git
```

This will give you the latest version for your system.

If you prefer to install git from the official site, you can do that, too. Head over to https://git-scm.com, click the download button, and follow the instructions.

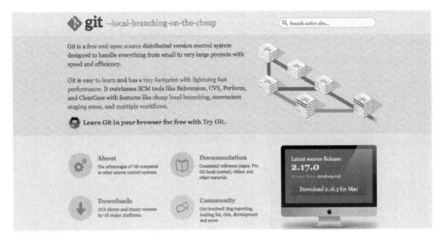

Node

Next, tackle node. There are three ways to install node. Each is valid and has its own positives and negatives. I will try to give you enough information for you to make an intelligent choice. Review them and choose the one you prefer.

If you like installing items from their source, feel free to head over to https://nodejs.org and click the big green button. The tools you are going to be using require at least Node 8, so you should not have any issues here. I recommend downloading and installing the LTS, or long-term-support version.

Node (Homebrew)

You can also use Homebrew to install node. Simply enter the following command in a terminal window.

```
brew install node
```

While it is installing, I would like to point out a few things that you will be seeing. The first thing Homebrew tries to do is update its local indexes. This is how it knows what software is available. The massive amount of text that fills the screen are all the new or updated software packages that Homebrew has been found since the last time it was run on this system.

Homebrew then finds node and its dependencies. It continues to download and install the dependencies, and finally, it installs node itself.

After not too long, depending on your internet connection, node is installed.

Note that the version of Node that gets installed should be the latest version available. You could have changed the brew command to specify a different version. And you are still stuck with just a single version of node, which may or may not be what you need all the time.

Fortunately, there is a better way, which I describe in detail later.

Linux Quick Start

If you plan to follow along on Linux, the tools should be straightforward

These steps were tested on Ubuntu Desktop 18.10, Cosmic Cuttlefish, which uses Debian packages. If you use a different version of Linux, you will need to alter these steps to work with your distribution's package manager.

There are two things you need to install: Node and Git.

There are three ways to install node. Each is valid and has its own its own positives and negatives. I will try to give you enough information for you to make an intelligent choice. Review them and choose the one you prefer.

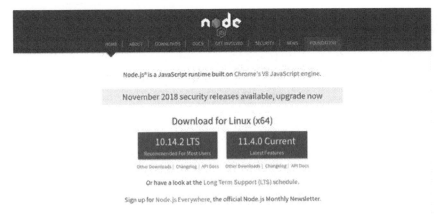

The first method is to download directly from nodejs.org itself. Quite frankly, I do not recommend this method. However, if you

like installing items from their official locations, feel free to head over to https://nodejs.org and click the big green button. I recommend downloading and installing the LTS, or long-term-support version.

Another way is to install node from the Ubuntu command line. Open a terminal window and type

```
node --version
```

to see if you already have it. In my pristine system, I do not. But Ubuntu tells me exactly how to get it.

To install it, simply enter the command provided, which should be

```
sudo apt-get install node
```

and it gets installed.

Now when you type node --version, you should see that the default Ubuntu version was installed. In my case, I got 8.10. So that is the second way, and it is better than the first, though you probably are not getting the LTS version. Fortunately, there is a third method, which is far more flexible. I describe that in the next section.

Node Version Manager

Now review another way to install Node on macOS and Linux. My preferred approach to anything relating to node and npm is to install a tool called the Node Version Manager, or nvm. It is a little more involved, but far more flexible overall.

What is nvm? It is an elegant set of shell script functions to enable the most flexible use of node imaginable.

The primary purpose of nvm is to enable you to install and switch between multiple versions of node and npm instantly. So, if you happen to have one project that requires Node 8, but another one that requires Node 4, for example, it is easy to keep them both installed, yet still independent from one another.

To me, the more notable features of nvm revolve around root, or administrator access. Many npm package installation instructions you will find on the web instruct you to use the sudo (or super-user do) command to install packages globally. It is possible that you may not have root access to your Mac, making those instructions worthless. There are workarounds, naturally, and they work fine. I used such workarounds for a few years before a colleague showed me nvm. Now I am convinced.

Once you commit to nvm, there is no reason ever to use sudo. In fact, you do not even need root access to install nvm. Everything gets installed under your own user account.

On macOS, install nvm with this command. It uses Homebrew, which you should now have.

```
brew install nvm
```

If you are on Linux, use this command, as these tools should exist on a stock Linux system.

```
wget -qO- https://raw.githubusercontent.com/nvm-sh/nvm/v0.35.3/install.sh | bash
```

One you have installed nvm, you can use it to install any version of node that you want. In this case, you will install the latest stable version. Simply execute the commands shown here.

Command	Description
nvm install 'lts/*'	Download and install the latest long-term-support, or LTS, version of Node.
node --version	Determine which version of node is currently

nvm current	in use.
nvm ls	Determine which versions of node you have installed
nvm ls-remote	Determine what versions of node are available to you. Warning: It is an extensive list.
nvm install v10.15	Install any available version of node (the v is optional).
nvm use v12.4	Switch to another version of nvm you have installed (the v is optional)

From this point forward, all of node and every npm package you install globally will be placed in the .nvm directory inside of your home directory. You should never have to use sudo to install an npm package globally. You're welcome.

Install Ionic

Finally, you need to install Ionic. Fortunately, this step is identical no matter which OS you use. Simply open the terminal of your choice and enter the following command

```
npm install -g @ionic/cli
```

This command will download and install the Ionic Framework tooling globally (that is what the -g flag does). Once installed, this tooling, known as the Ionic CLI, provides a variety of commands to help you in your Ionic development. Some of the important commands are shown here.

Command	Description
ionic info	Prints project, system, and environment information.

ionic docs	Opens the Ionic documentation website.
ionic start	Creates a new project
ionic generate	Creates new project assets (pages, components, interfaces, services, etc.). Note, this command currently only supports Ionic-Angular projects.

Printed in Great Britain
by Amazon

48689124R00054